What is Prayer?

CAROLYN NYSTROM

Illustrated by
Wayne A. Hanna

MOODY PRESS
CHICAGO

to Joyce
who prays with me

© 1980 by
THE MOODY BIBLE INSTITUTE
OF CHICAGO

ISBN: 0-8024-5991-9

Printed in the United States of America

Moody Press, a ministry of the Moody Bible Institute,
is designed for education, evangelization, and
edification. If we may assist you in knowing more about
Christ and the Christian life, please write us without
obligation: Moody Press, c/o MLM, Chicago, Illinois 60610.

Have you ever talked to God? I have.
Prayer is so special that I want everyone to
know about it.

Romans 15:4

You see, God loves me so much
that He wants to talk to me. That's why He
gave me the Bible.

John 4:23

But God wants me to talk to Him too. So in
the Bible He tells me how to pray. Prayer
is talking to God.

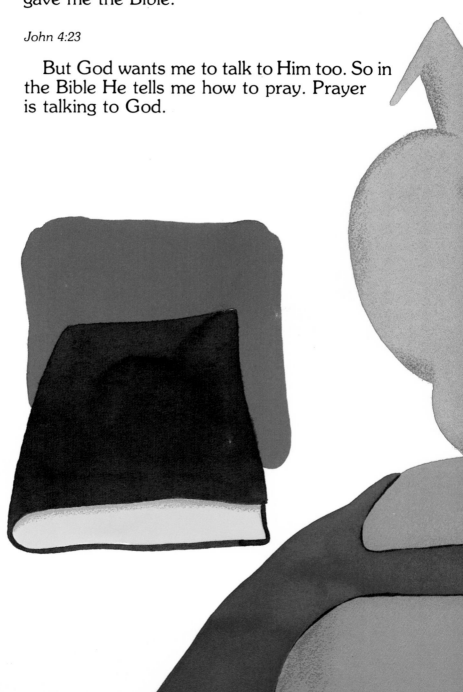

John 15:15

Friends like to talk to each other. And God is my friend.

Psalm 139:1-12

I can talk to God ANYWHERE about ANYTHING. God always hears and understands.

God hears me if I whisper, or if I shout,
or even if I only think a prayer in my mind.

I can pray when I run, when I sit, or when I stand. God still hears.

But sometimes I want God to see how I feel about my prayer. I might stand to show God that I respect Him.

Psalm 95:6; 134:1-2; 1 Timothy 2:8; 2 Samuel 6:14

I might kneel down to show God that I am sorry for doing wrong. I might let my whole body show God how happy I am to know Him. God sees and hears and knows what I mean.

Psalm 139:6

I read in the Bible about how great God is. He knows everything. He sees everywhere. He can do anything. And God loves me. I praise Him. I pray, "God, You are wonderful."

2 Corinthians 1:11

God makes Daddy strong and healthy so that he can work hard and buy me a shiny new bike.

I pray, "Thank You, God."

I thank Daddy too.

James 5:14-15

When my friend Bobby is sick, I ask God to make him well.
   I pray, "God, please help Bobby."
And He does.

When I think about going to school,
I worry about what sort of teacher I'll have.
I pray, "God, I'm scared. Please give me
a kind teacher."
And Miss Newman is just great.

But I don't always please God. I get angry
at Bobby. Or I tell my mother I've eaten all my
peas when I haven't. Or I won't play with
Suzy. Or I play too rough with my
puppy. God hates sin.

1 John 1:9

So I pray, "God, I'm sorry. I'll try not to do it again." And God forgives.

Romans 12:1

I want to show God how much I love Him.
I pray, "God, I give You a present. It is myself."

There are many kinds of prayer.
Sometimes I pray a short prayer about just
one thing. Other times I mix up all kinds
of prayers and talk to God a long time.

1 Thessalonians 5:17

God wants me to talk to Him often.
In the Bible, He says, "Pray without ceasing."
That means, "Always be ready
to pray."

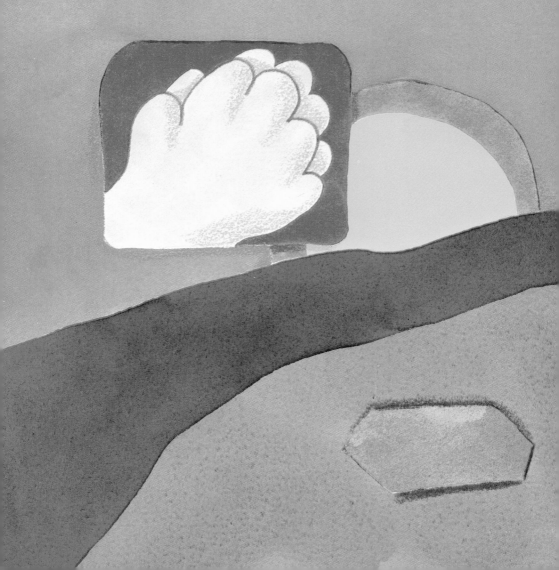

God wants me to pray sometimes with other people. The Bible tells me prayer has great power when two or three pray together.

God knew I'd want to please Him with my prayers. So in the Bible He gave rules for praying. He said: Don't say lots of words that don't mean anything. Don't say the same thing over and over for no reason. Don't pray just to show off.

Matthew 6:9-13

When Jesus was here, He prayed often. Once Jesus' followers asked Him to teach them to pray too. He told them, "Pray like this."

*"Our Father which art in heaven,
    Hallowed be thy name.*

*Thy kingdom come. Thy will
    be done in earth, as it is
    in heaven.*

Give us this day our daily bread.

*And forgive us our debts,
    as we forgive our debtors.*

*And lead us not into temptation,
    but deliver us from evil:*

*For thine is the kingdom,
    and the power, and the glory,
    for ever.   Amen."*

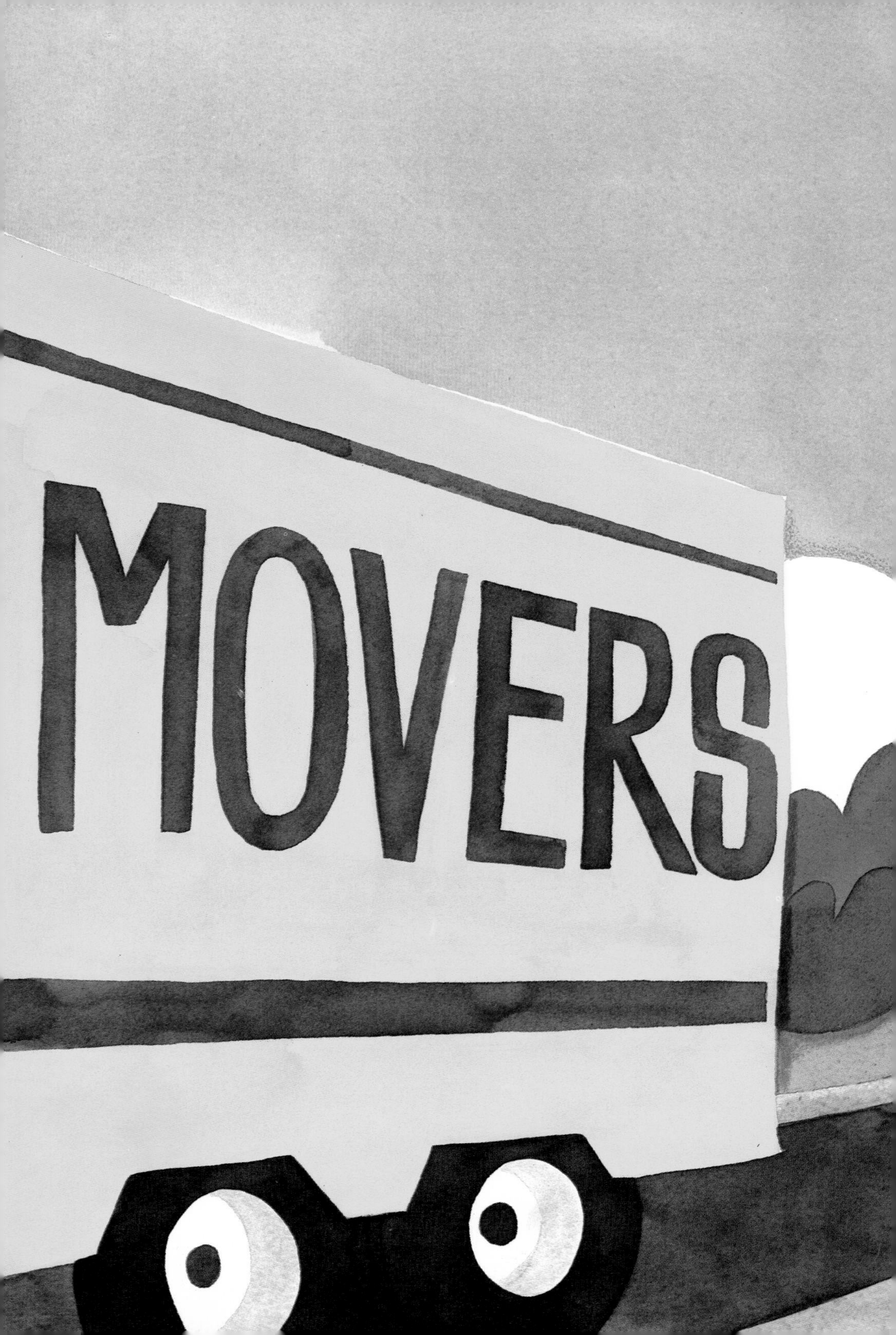
MOVERS

Even if I'm not sure how to pray,
God wants me to pray anyway. The Holy Spirit
will make my prayer right.

But sometimes I ask God for something
that He does not give. Once I asked God
to keep my best friend, Linda, from moving
away. But Linda moved anyway.

So I wondered, *Did God hear? Did God care how much I wanted Linda to stay? Did I ask something too hard for God?*

Then I remembered, *God hears. God cares. And there is nothing too hard for God.* And I remembered other times when He answered my prayers. I thanked Him for those times.

Matthew 17:20

God gives me some reasons in the Bible—reasons why He does not always give what I ask.

Perhaps I don't really believe that God will answer my prayer. I need to trust Him more.

Maybe I am angry at someone who has done wrong to me. I need to make up with him.

Or I might be doing something that displeases God. I need to turn away from that sin and tell God I'm sorry.

But most likely, God knows that what I ask is not good for me—or for someone else. And God knows best. I don't want God to give me what I ask if He knows it isn't good.

Maybe God knows it was better for Linda to move away. God knows I feel sad. I can tell Him how I feel.

God hears every prayer. And God wants to give me good things. But He wants me to ask Him. It shows I need and trust Him.

God is so big and so good and so wonderful. And He is my friend. He wants me to talk to Him. That's why I pray.

You can pray too.
God wants to be your friend.